Hues

the colors of life

A COLORING BOOK

ISBN: 1727070720
ISBN-13: 978-1727070729

Cover and Interior Design & Illustrations by Kozakura
(www.fiverr.com/kozakura)

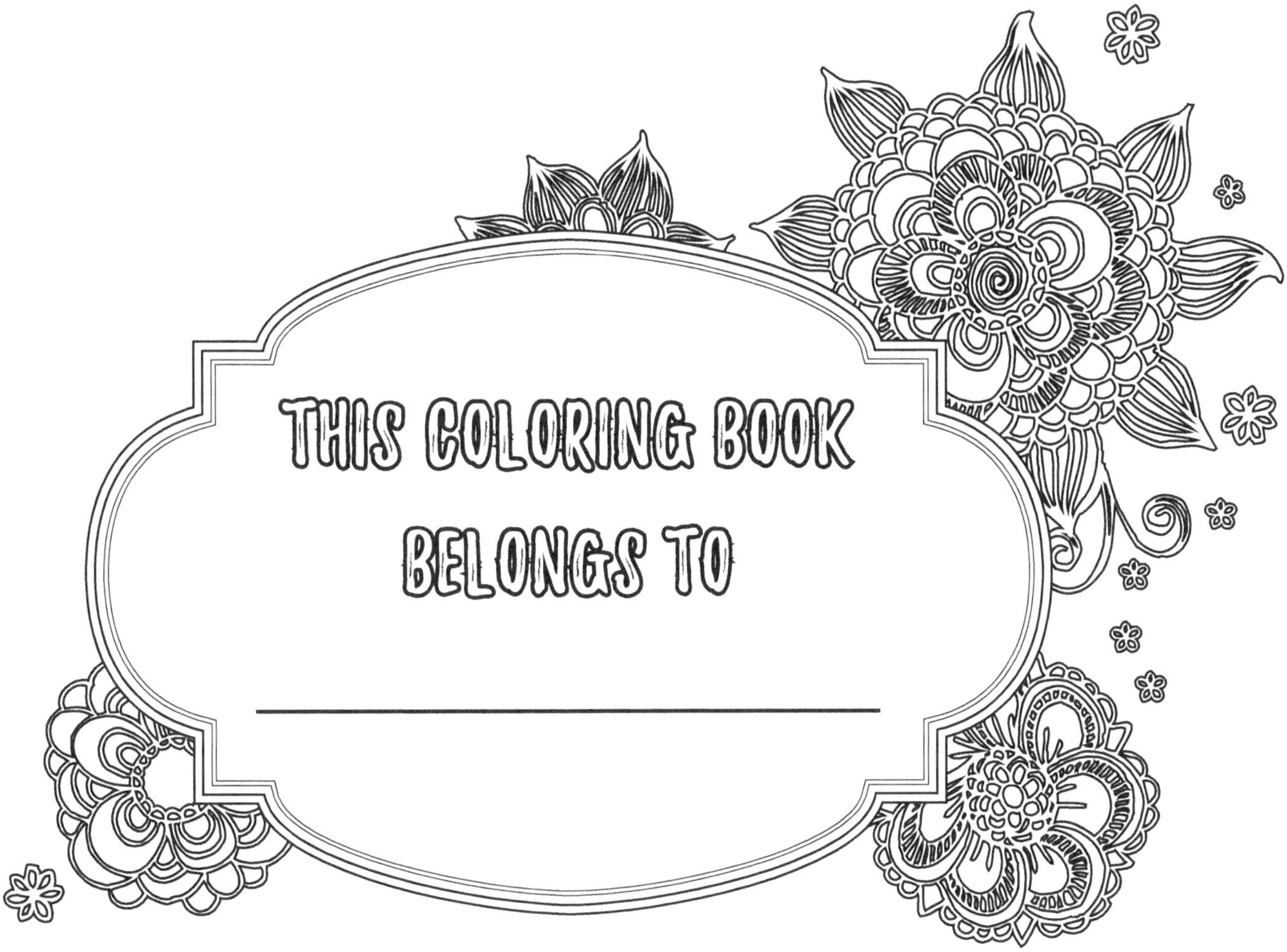
THIS COLORING BOOK
BELONGS TO

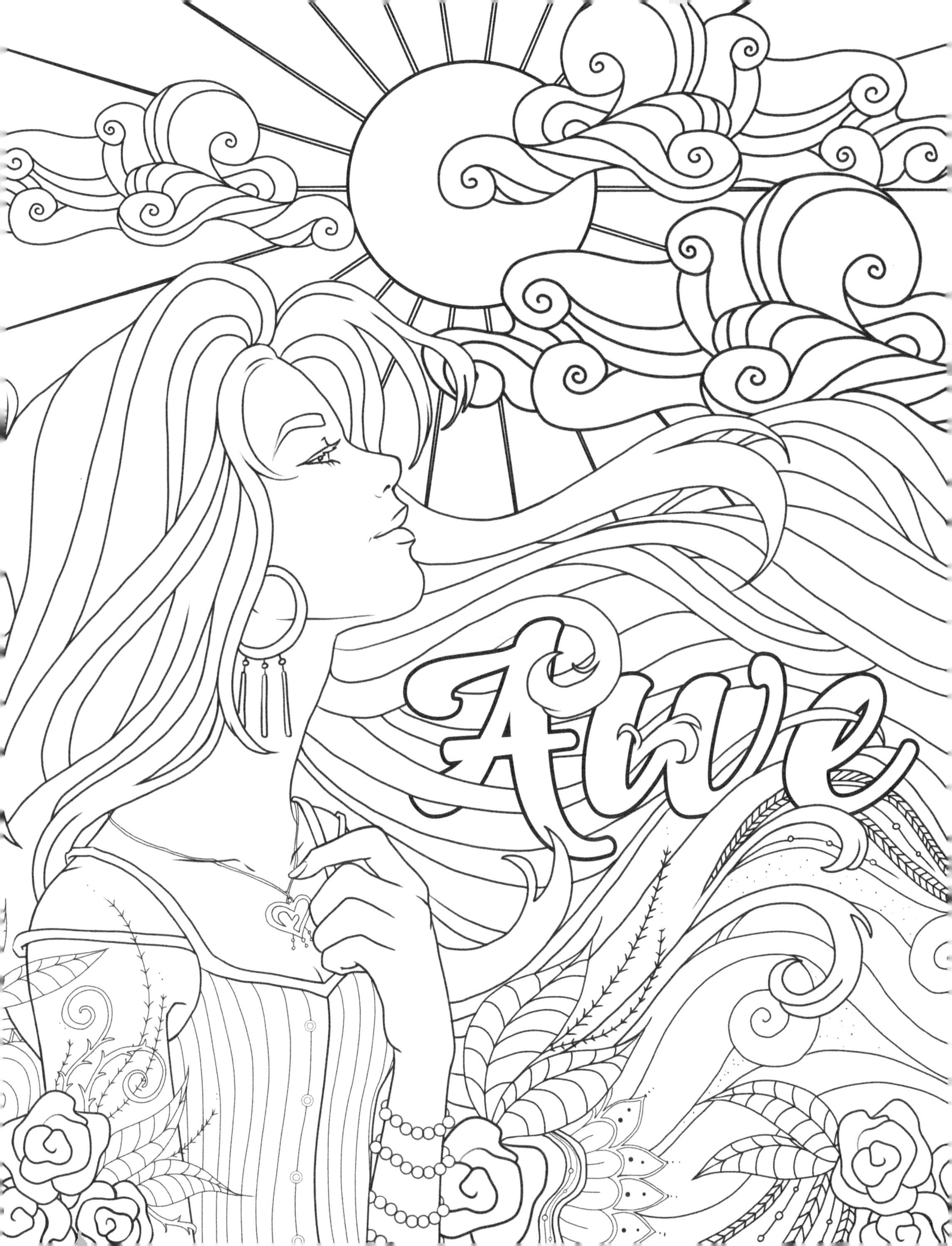
Awe

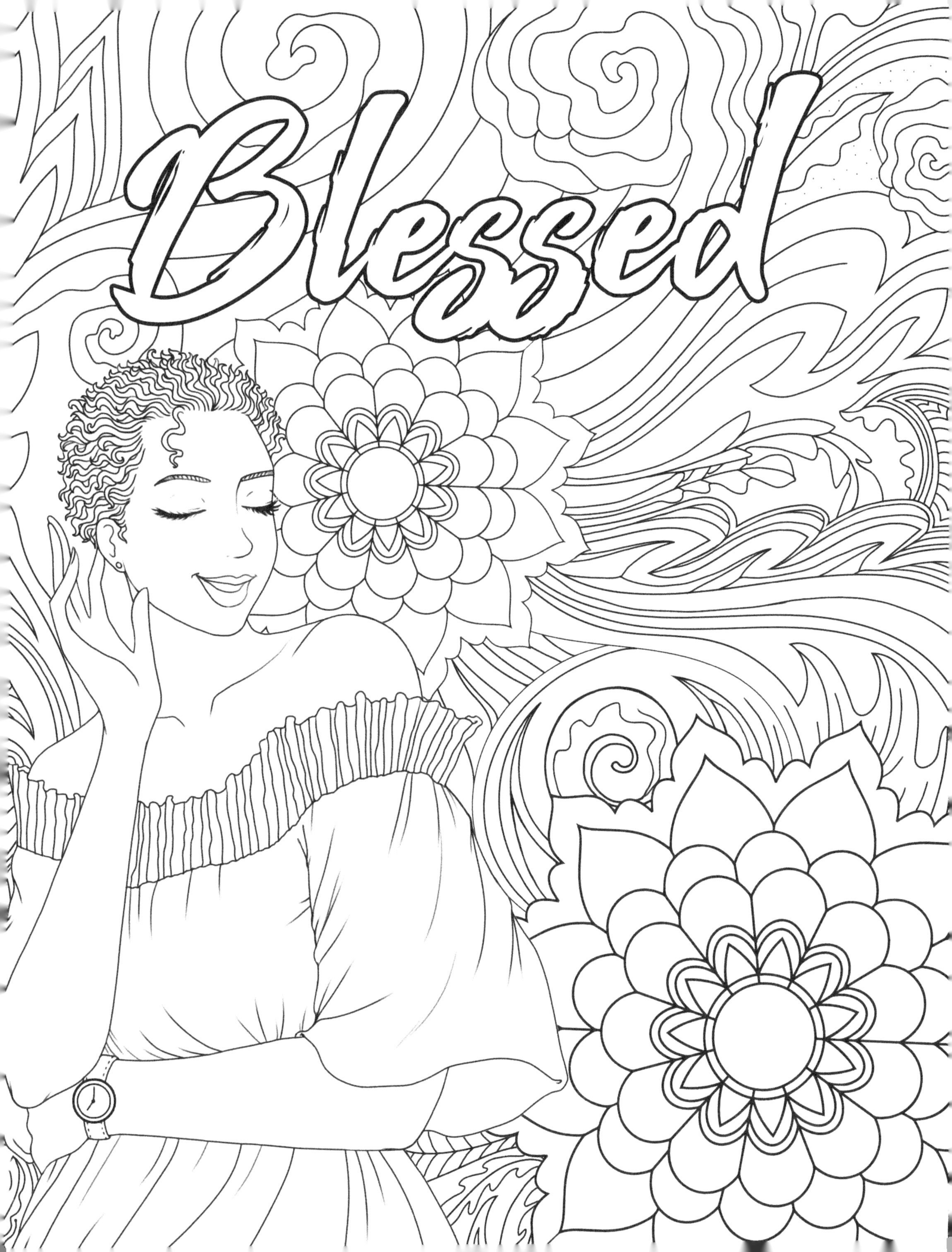
Blessed

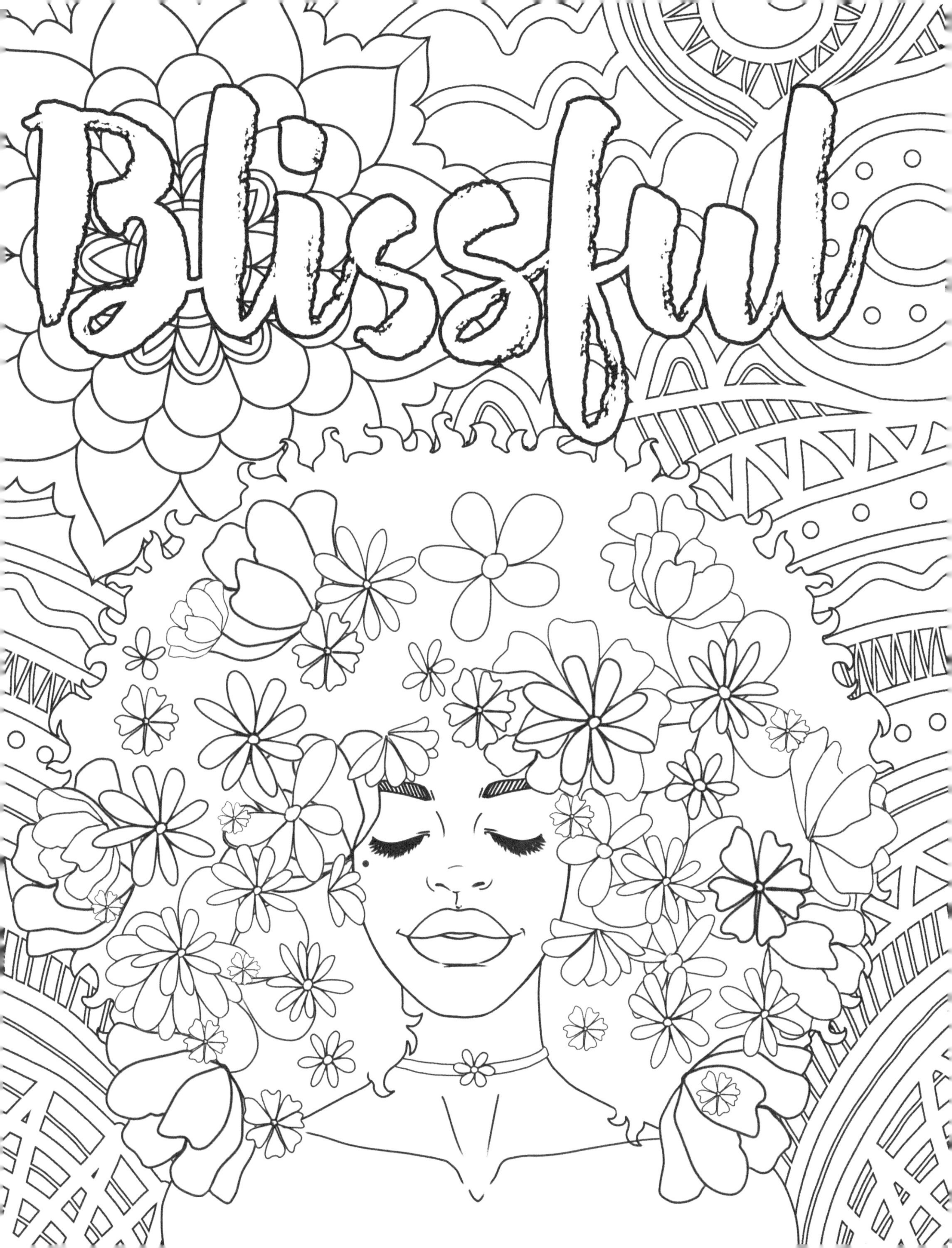
Blissful

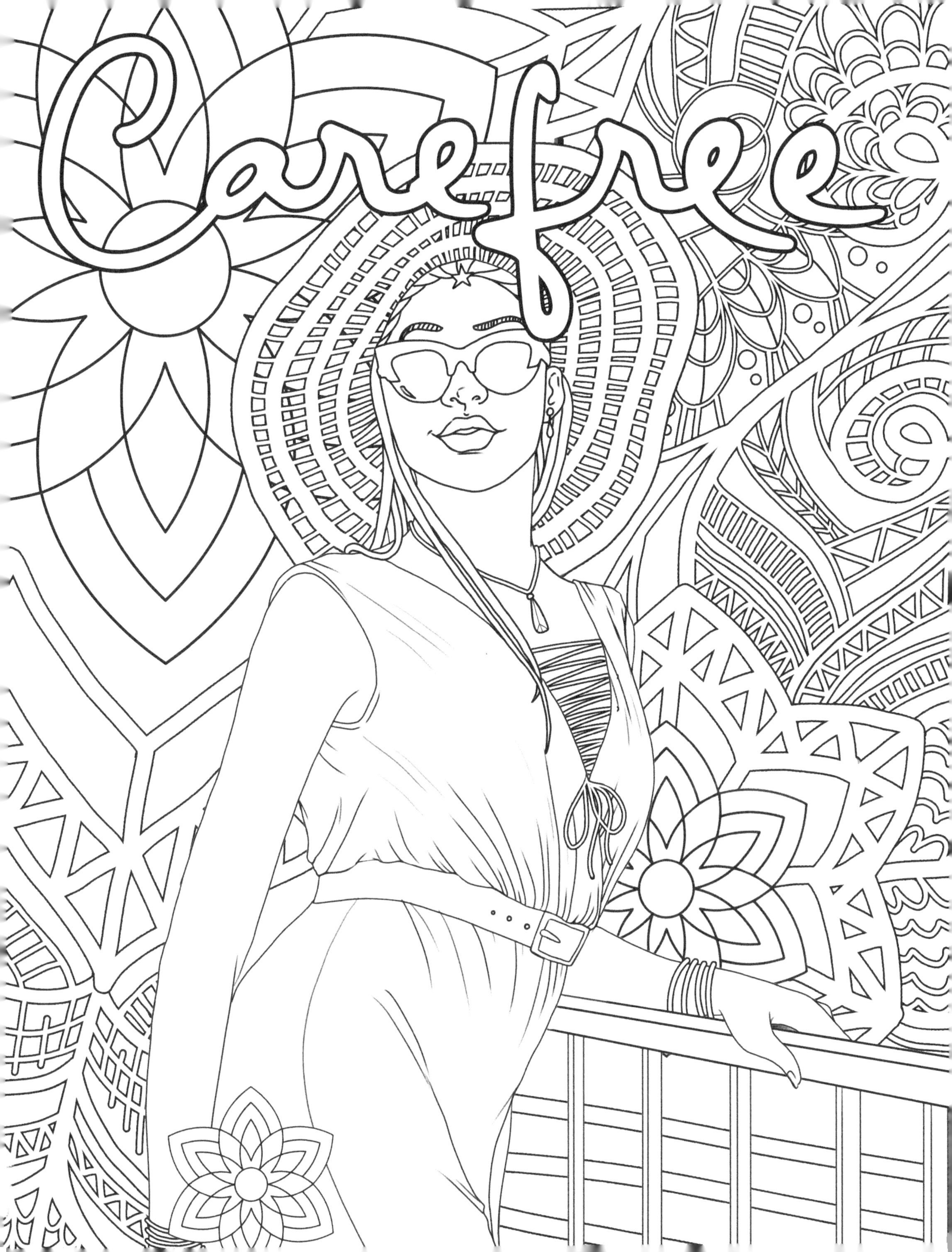
Carefree

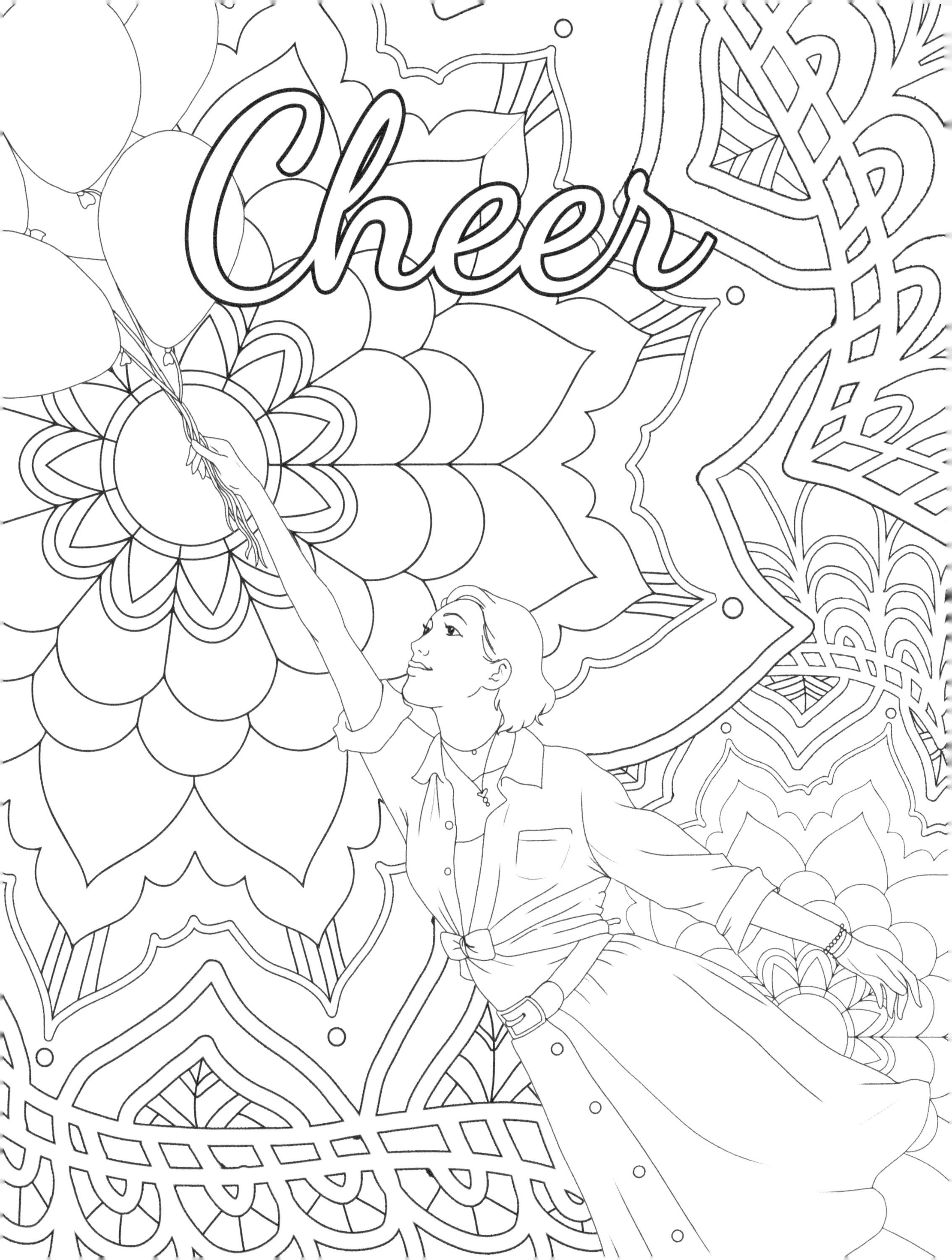
Cheer

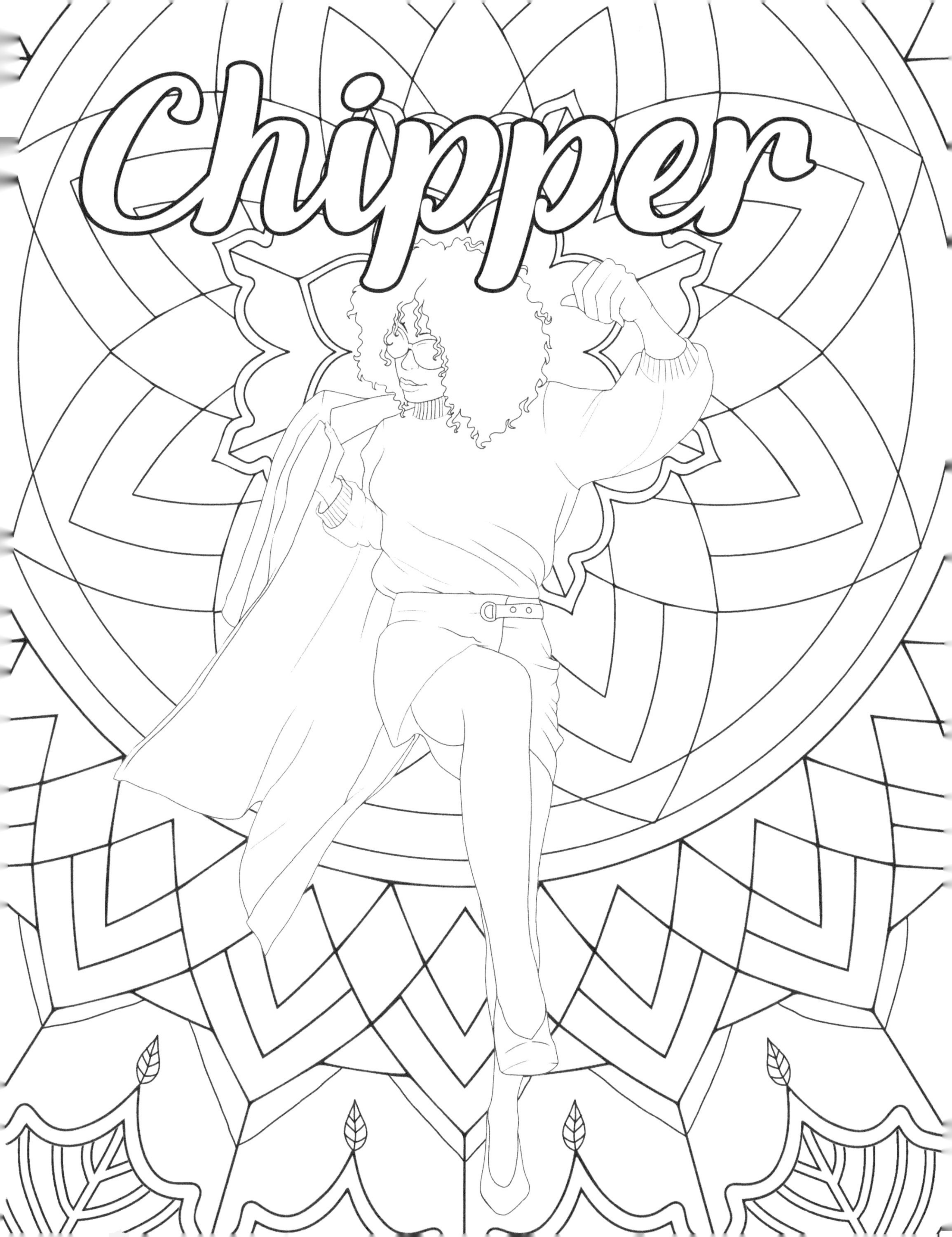
Chipper

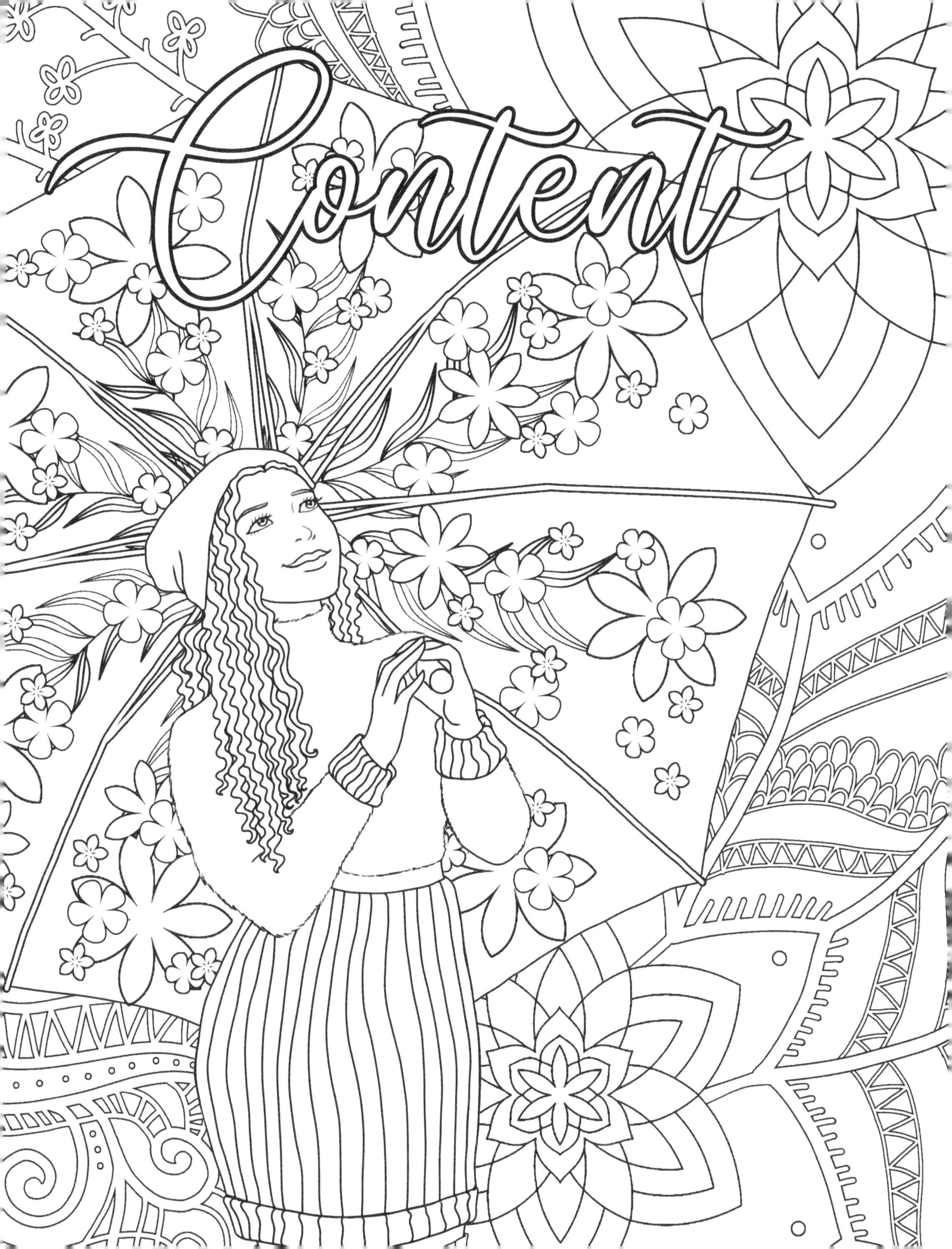
Content

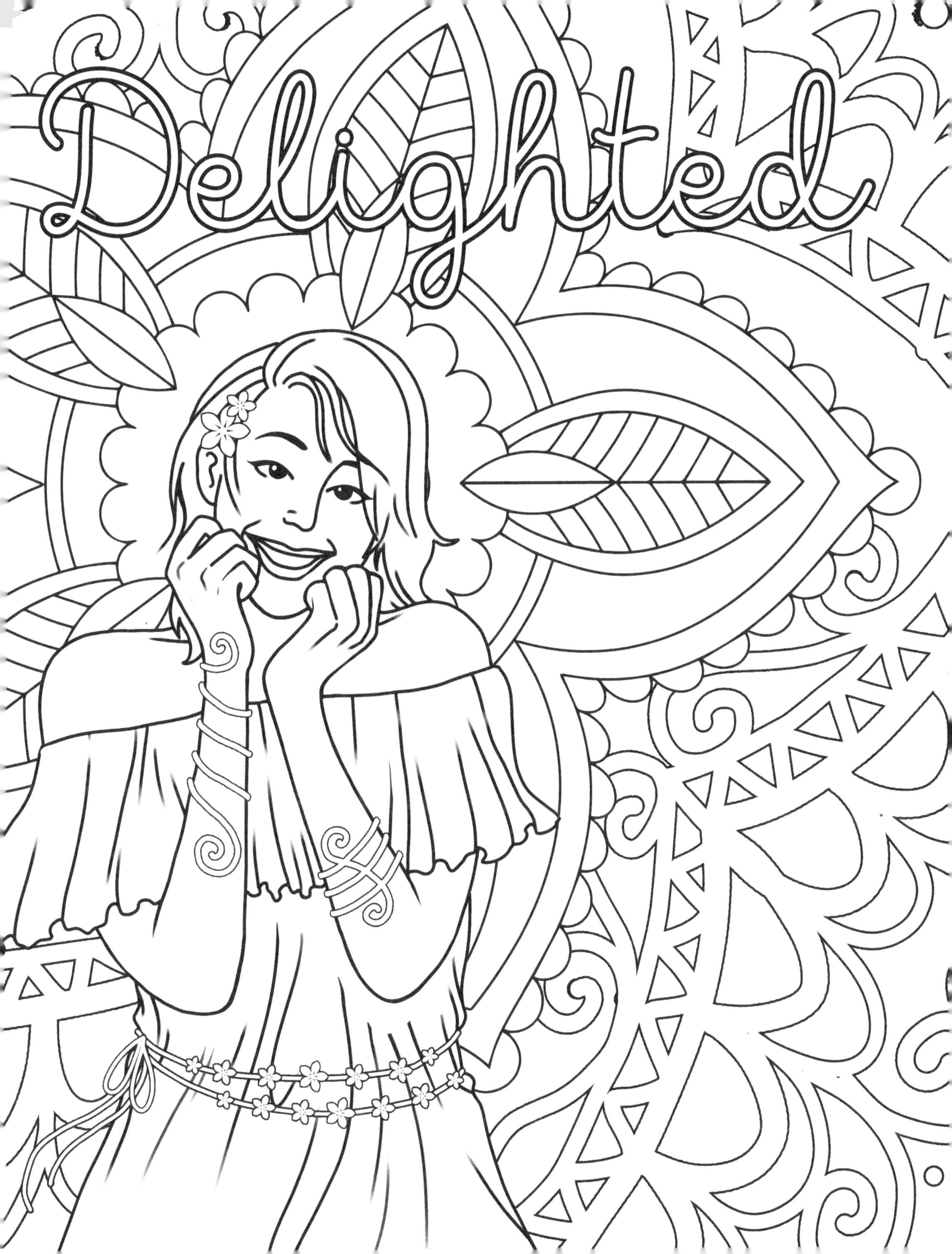
Delighted

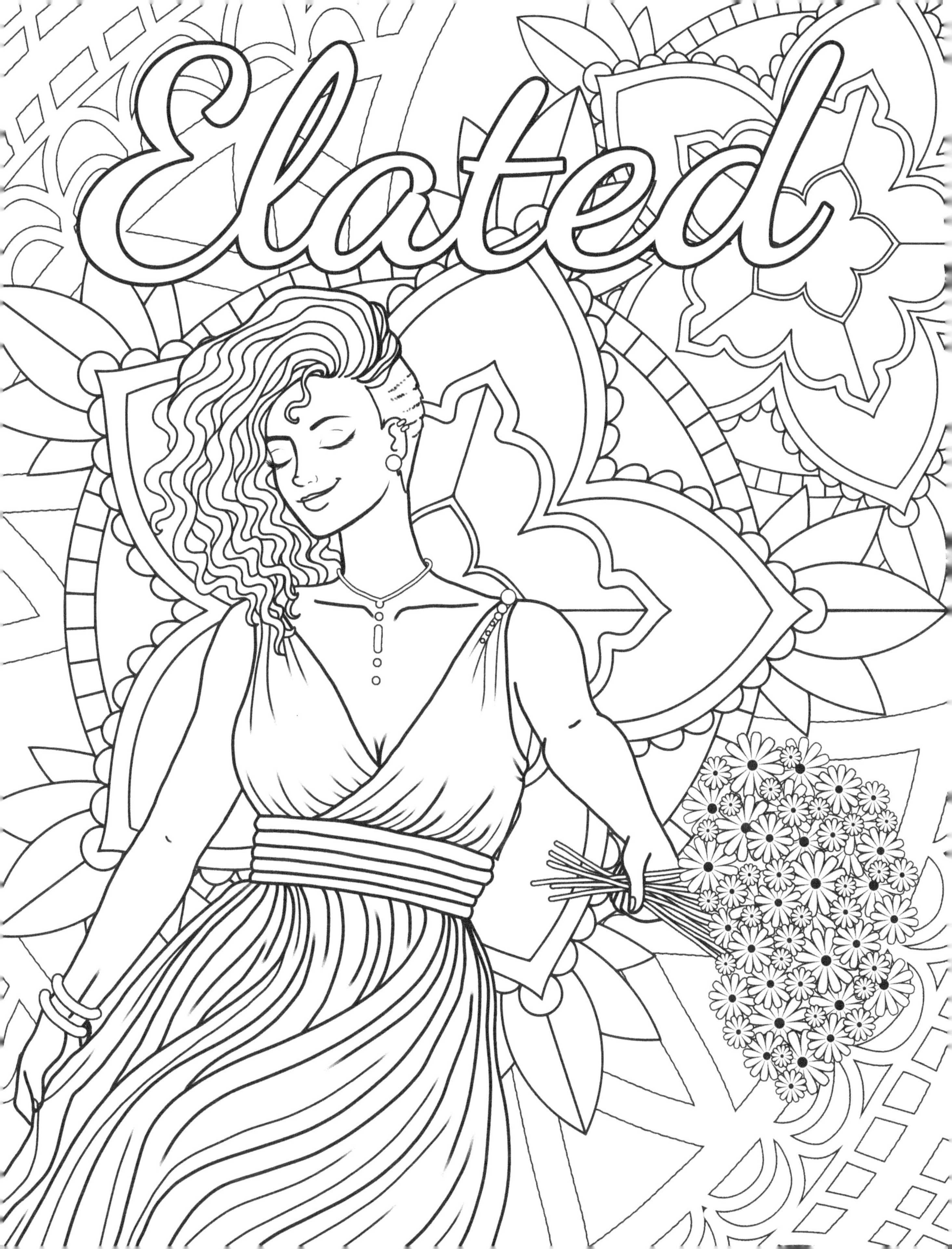
Elated

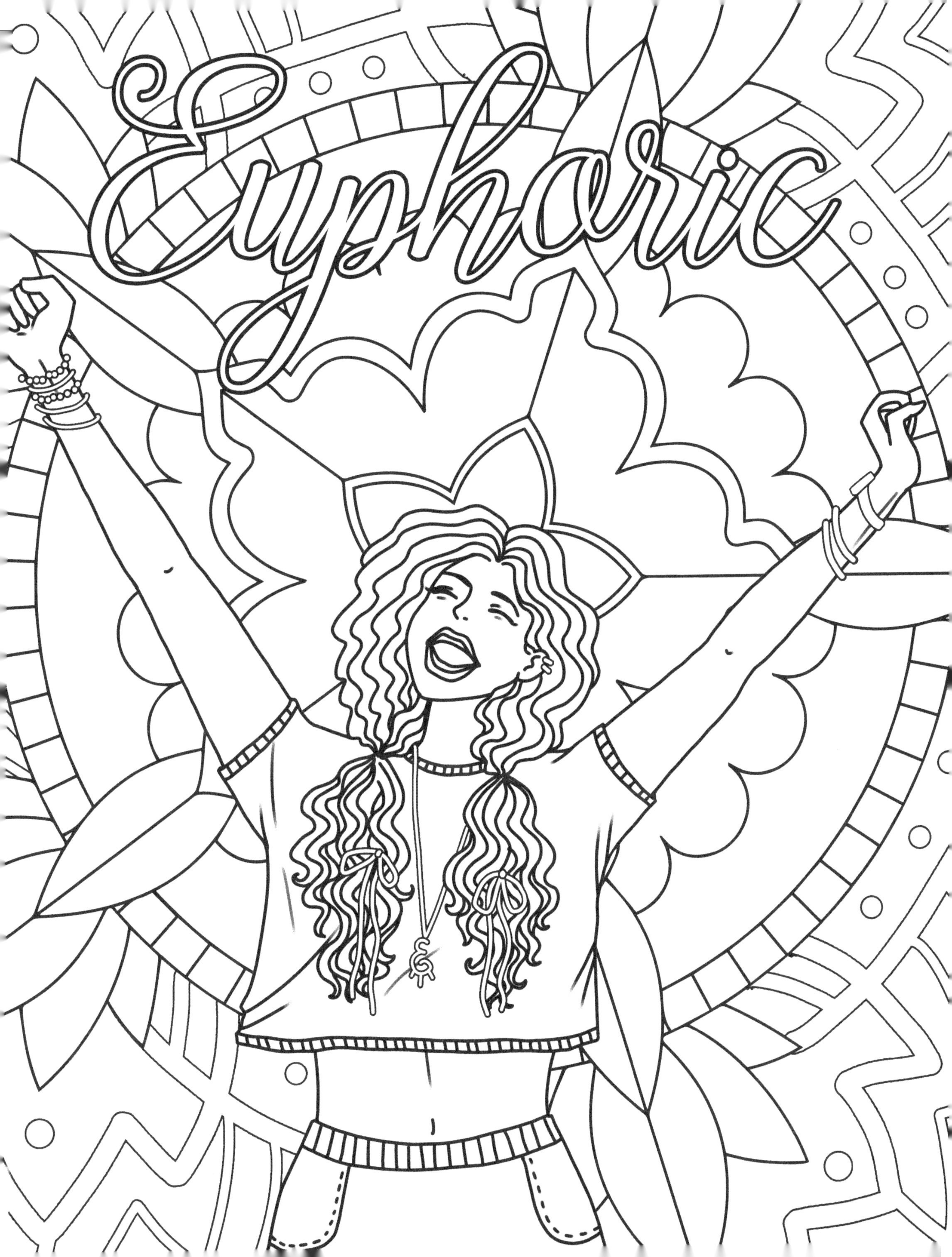
Euphoric

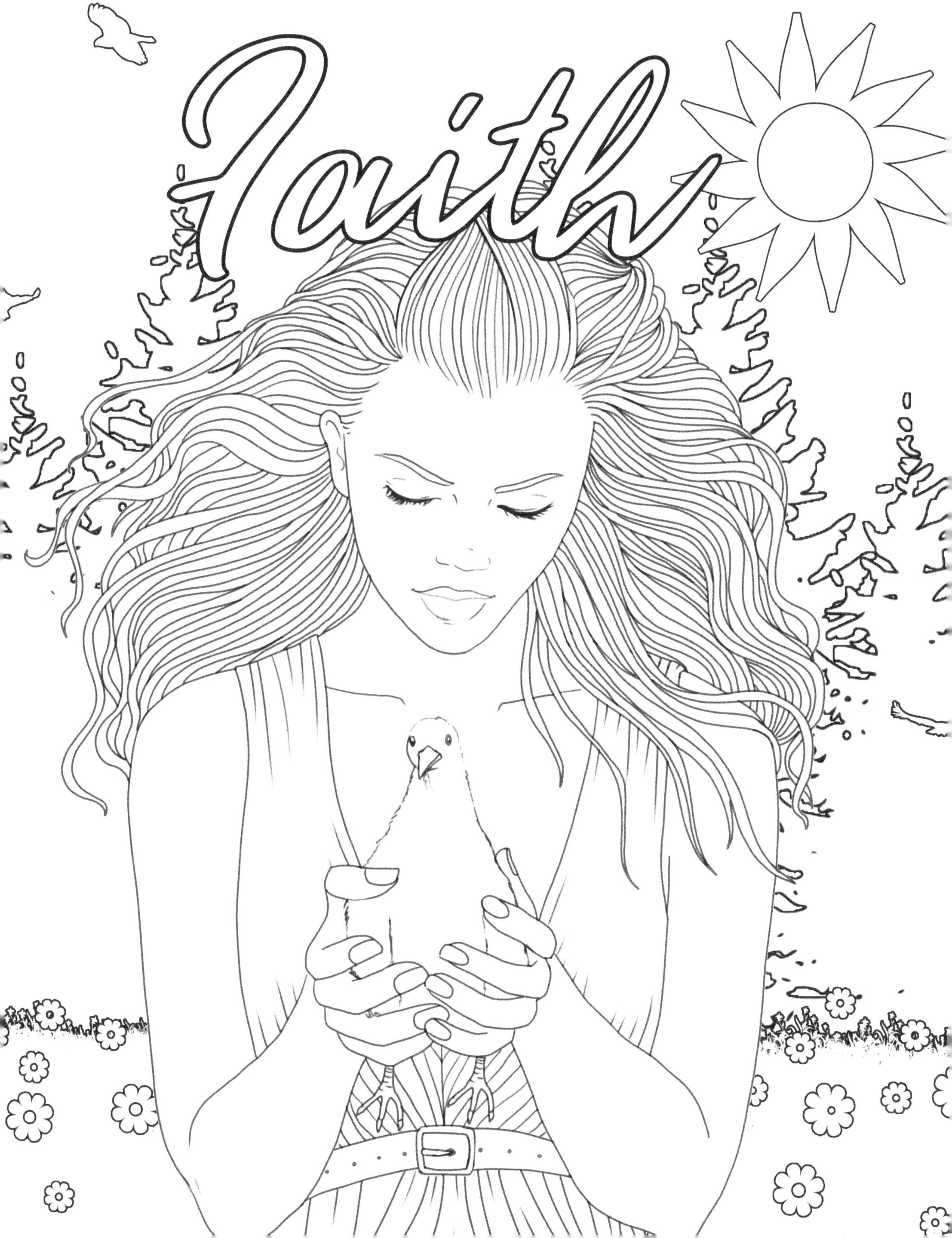
Faith

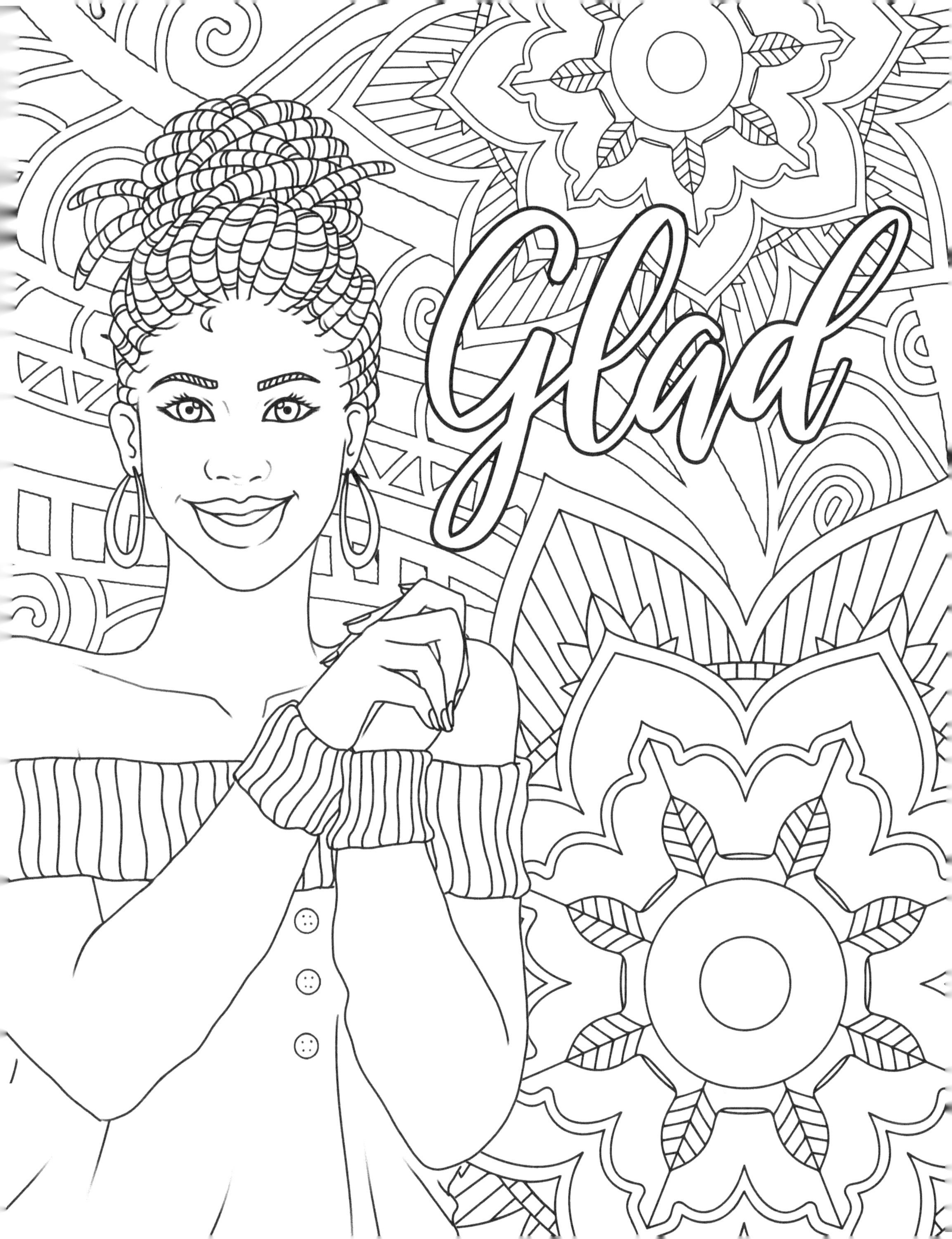
Glad

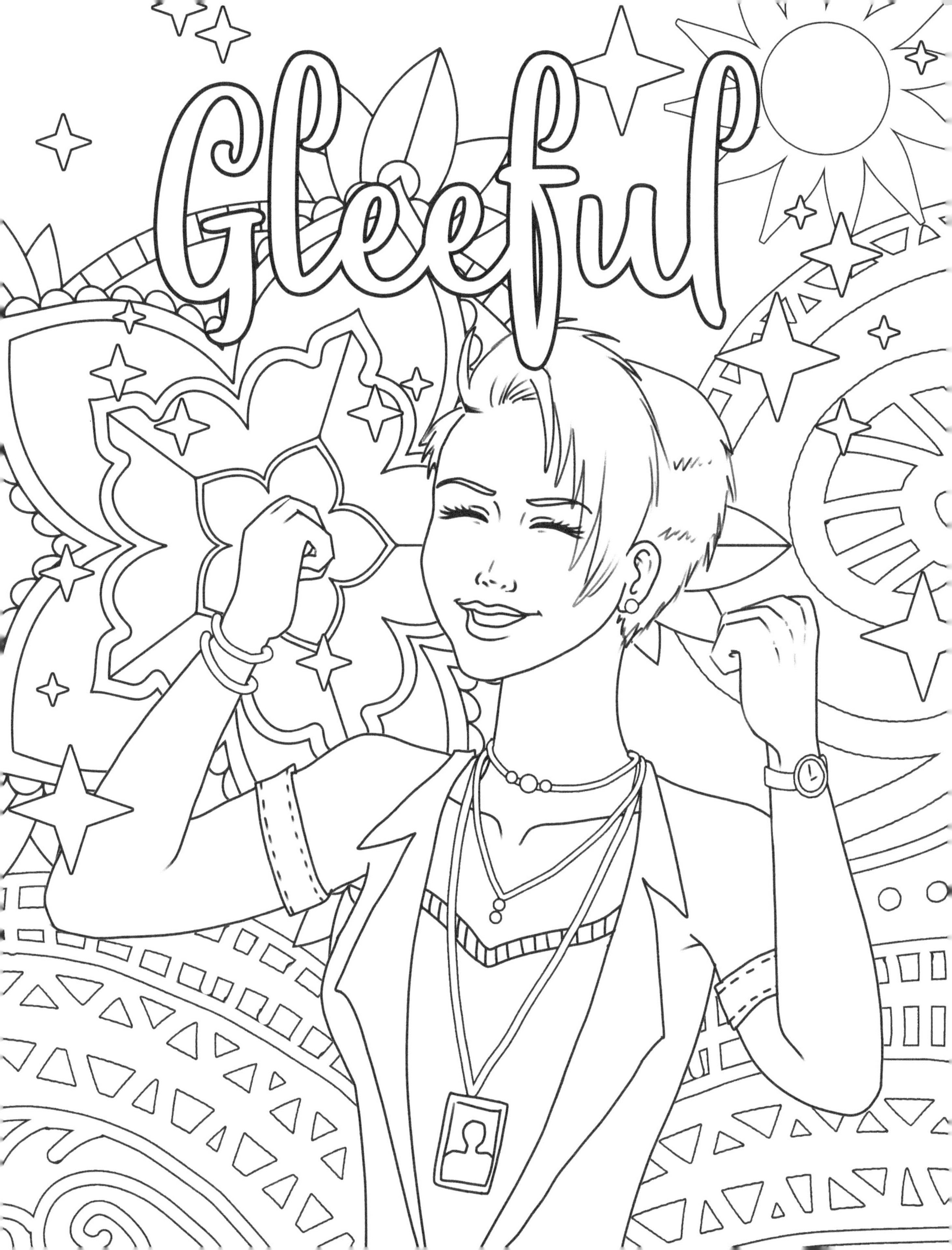
Gleeful

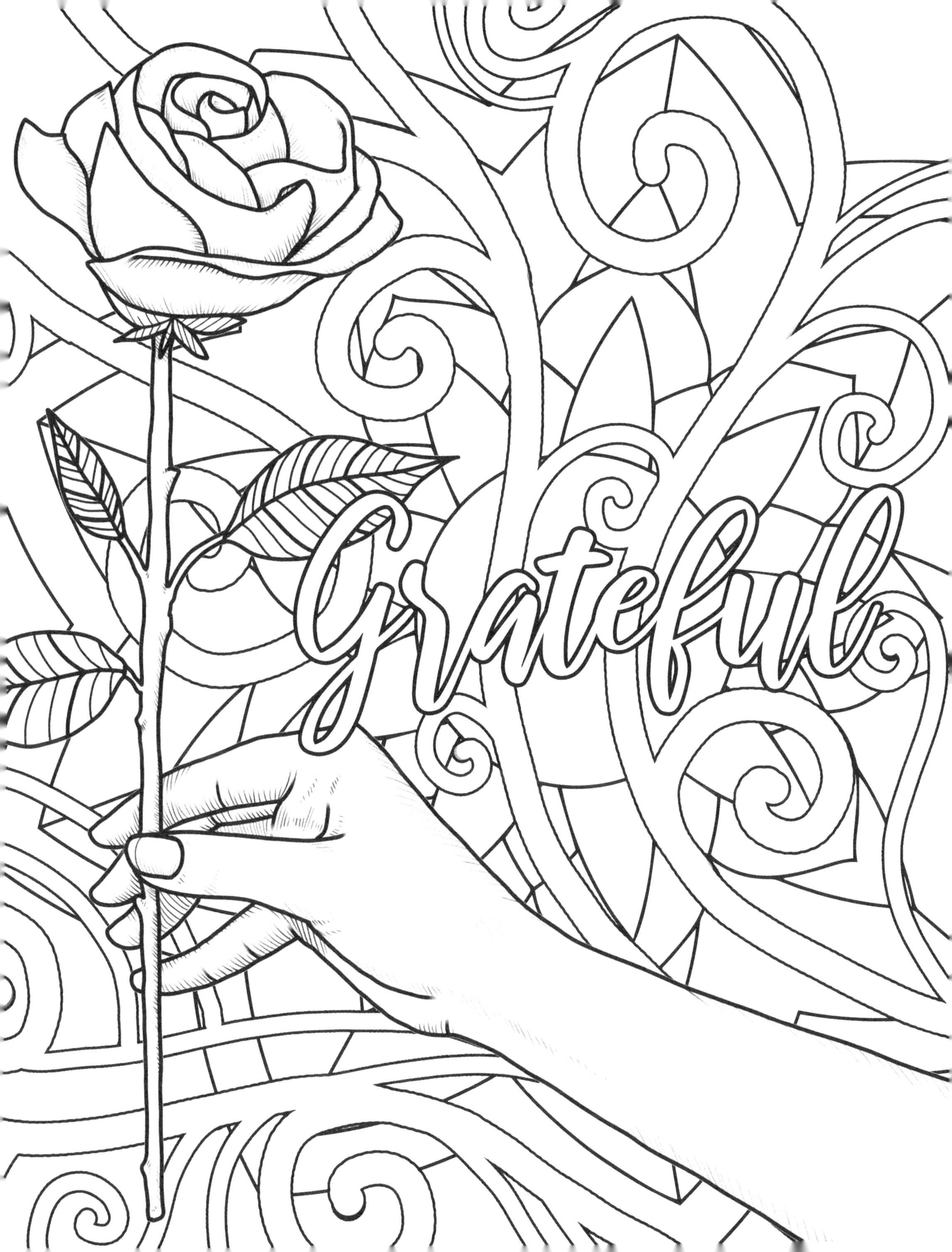
Grateful

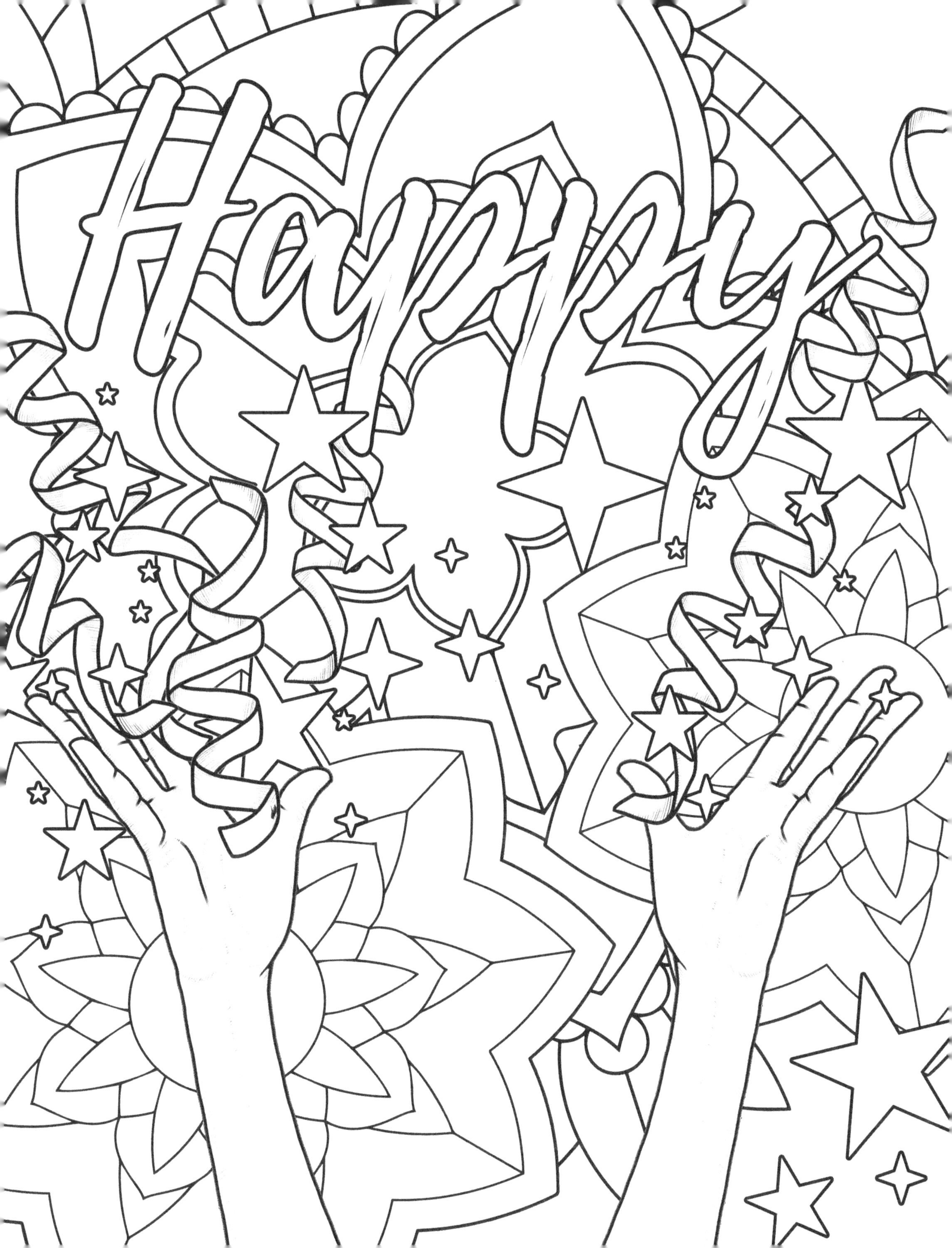
Happy

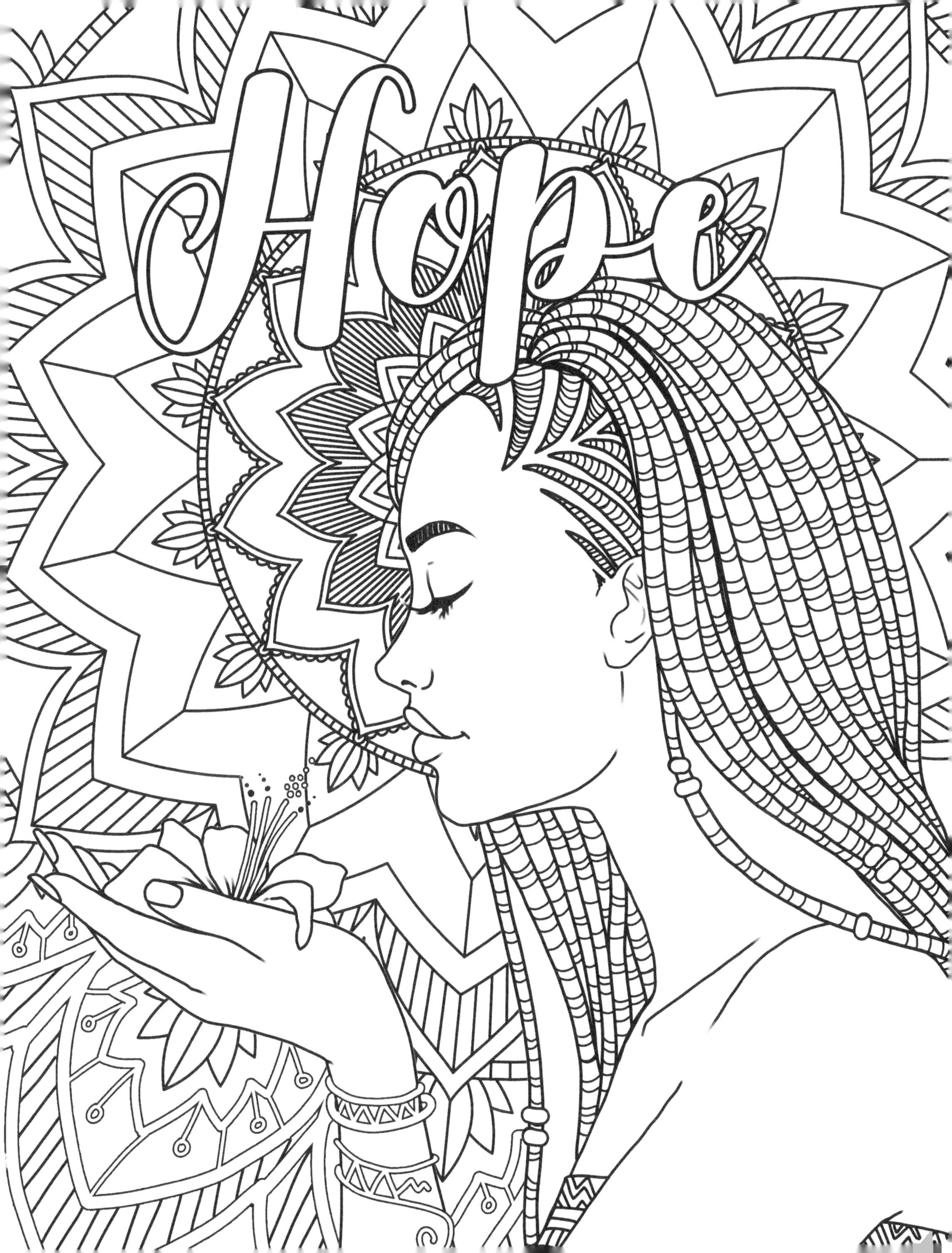
Hope

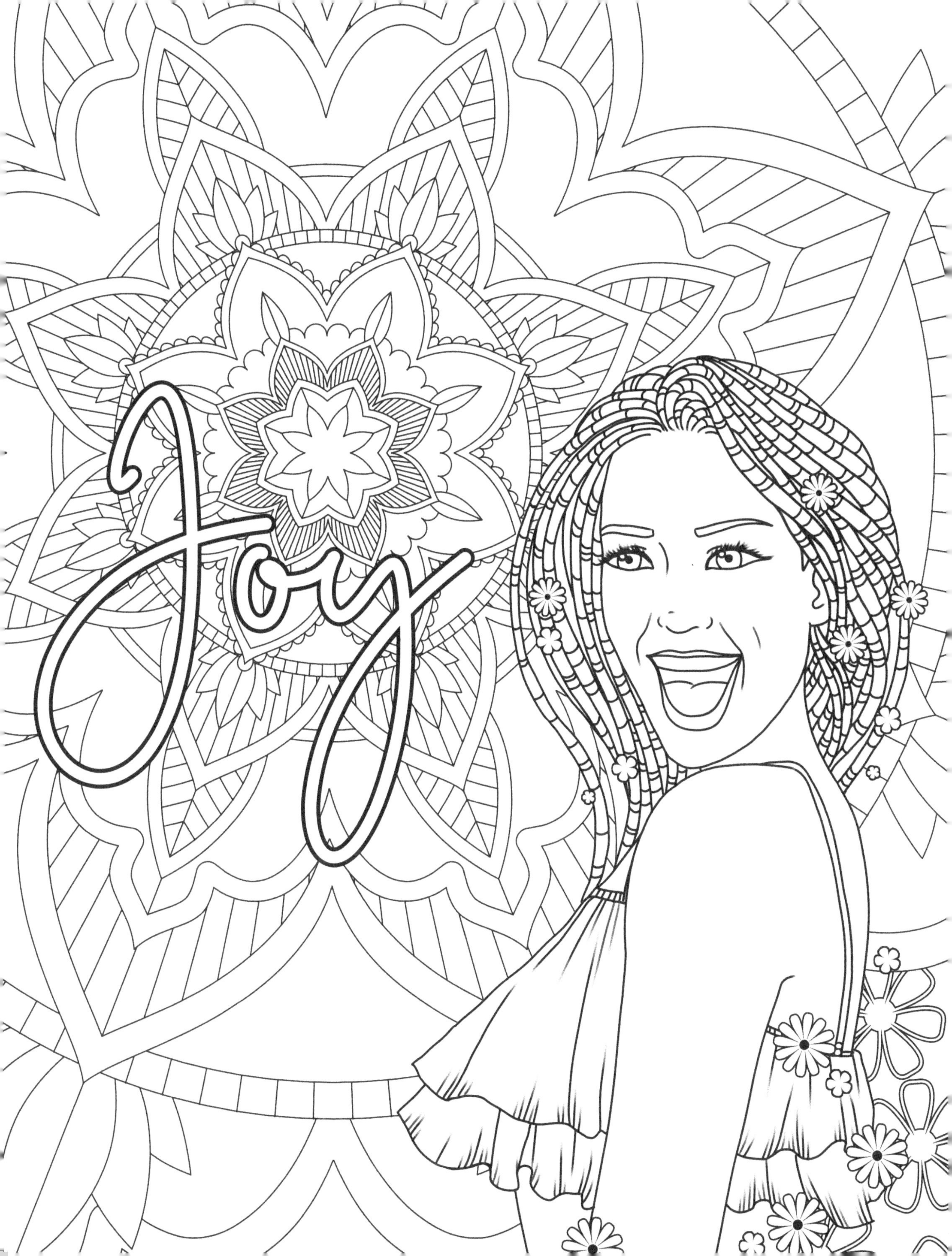
Joy

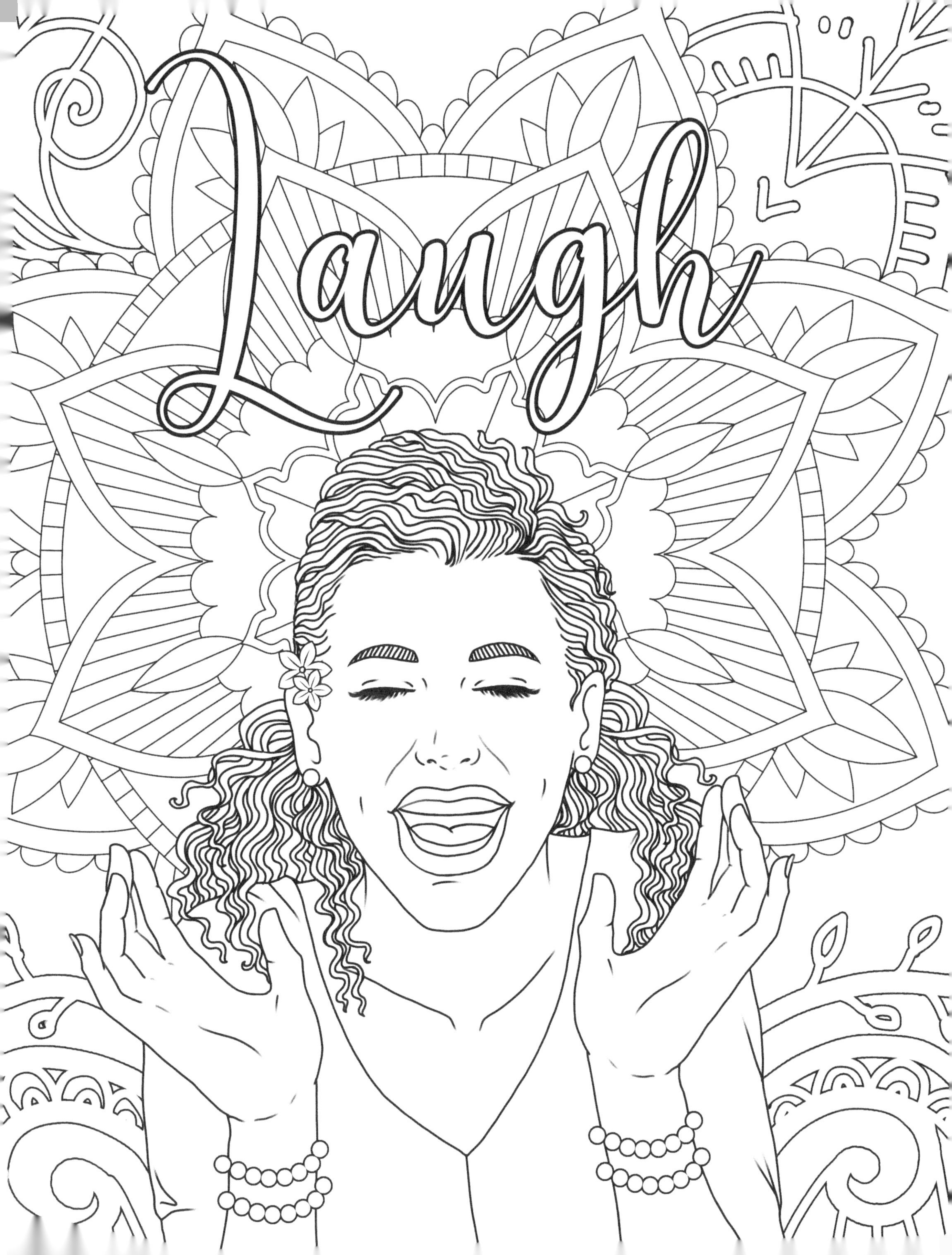
Laugh

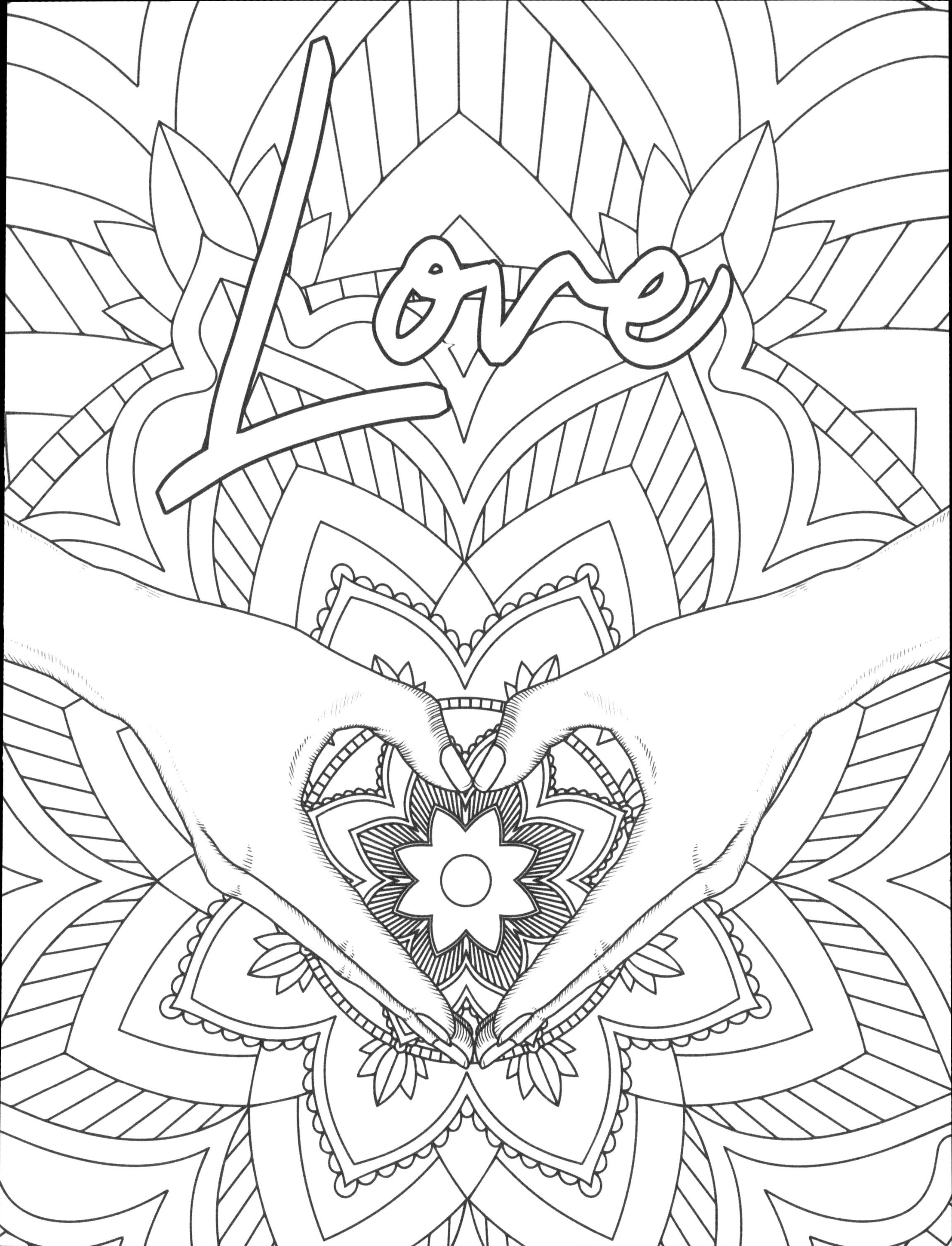
Love

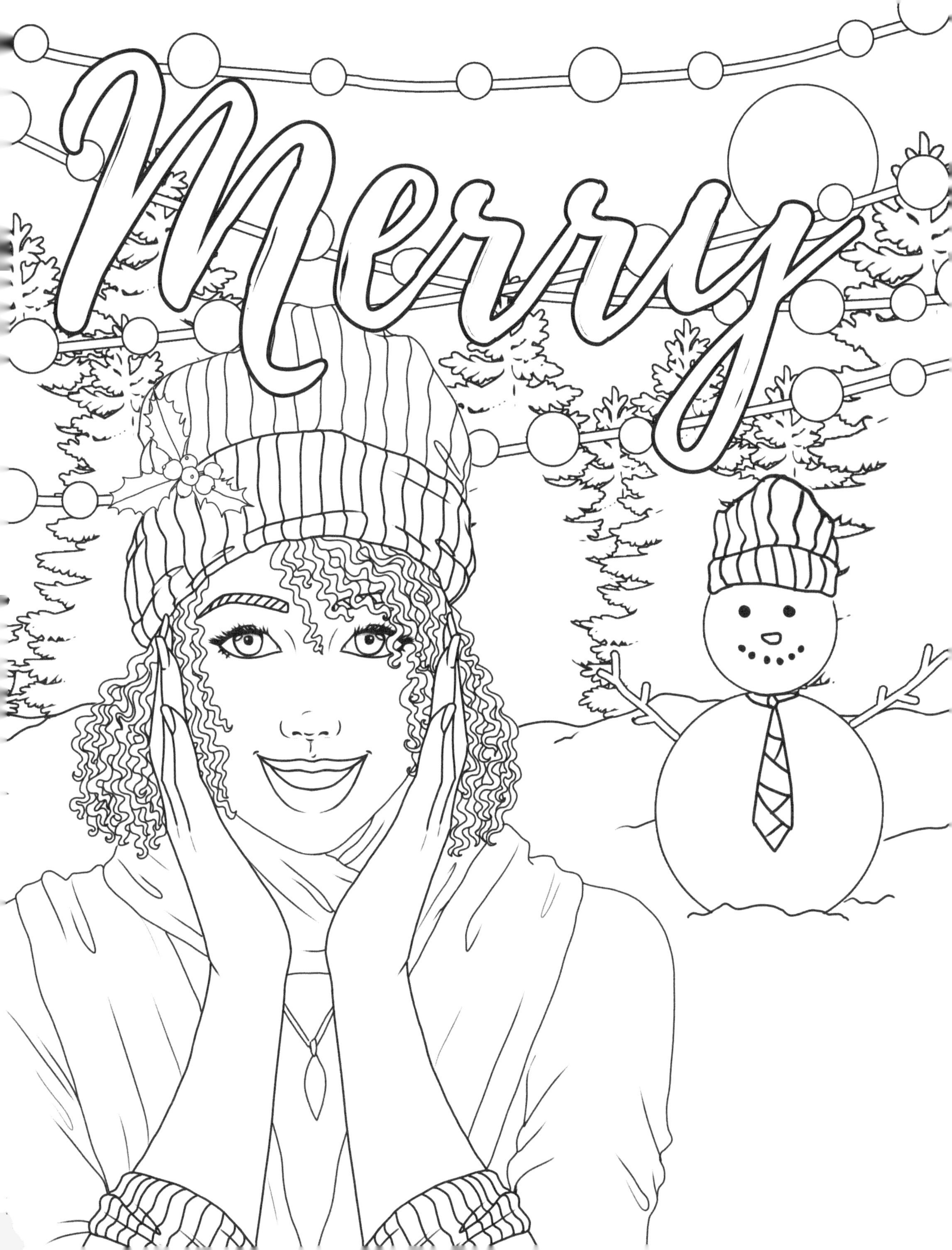
Merry

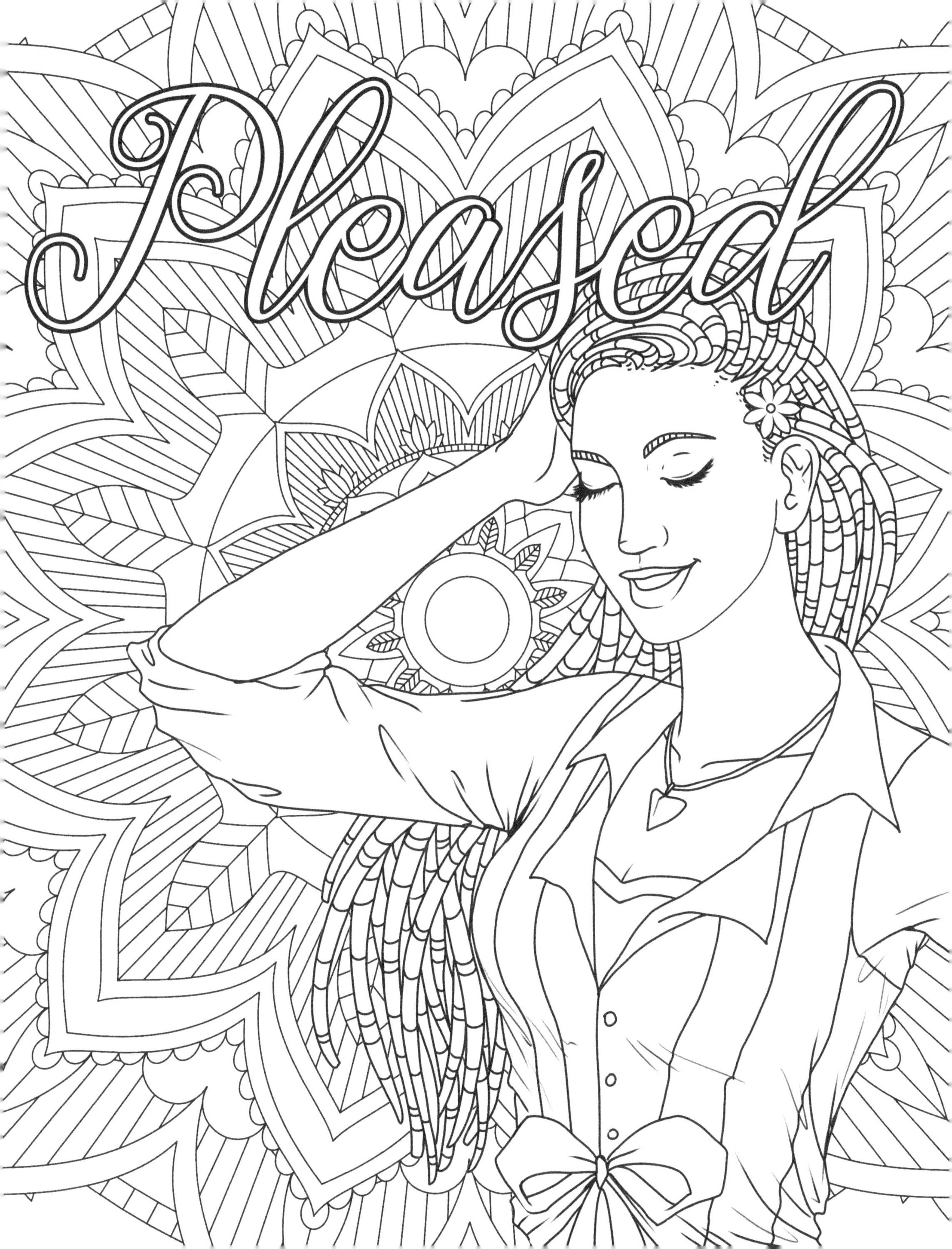
Pleased

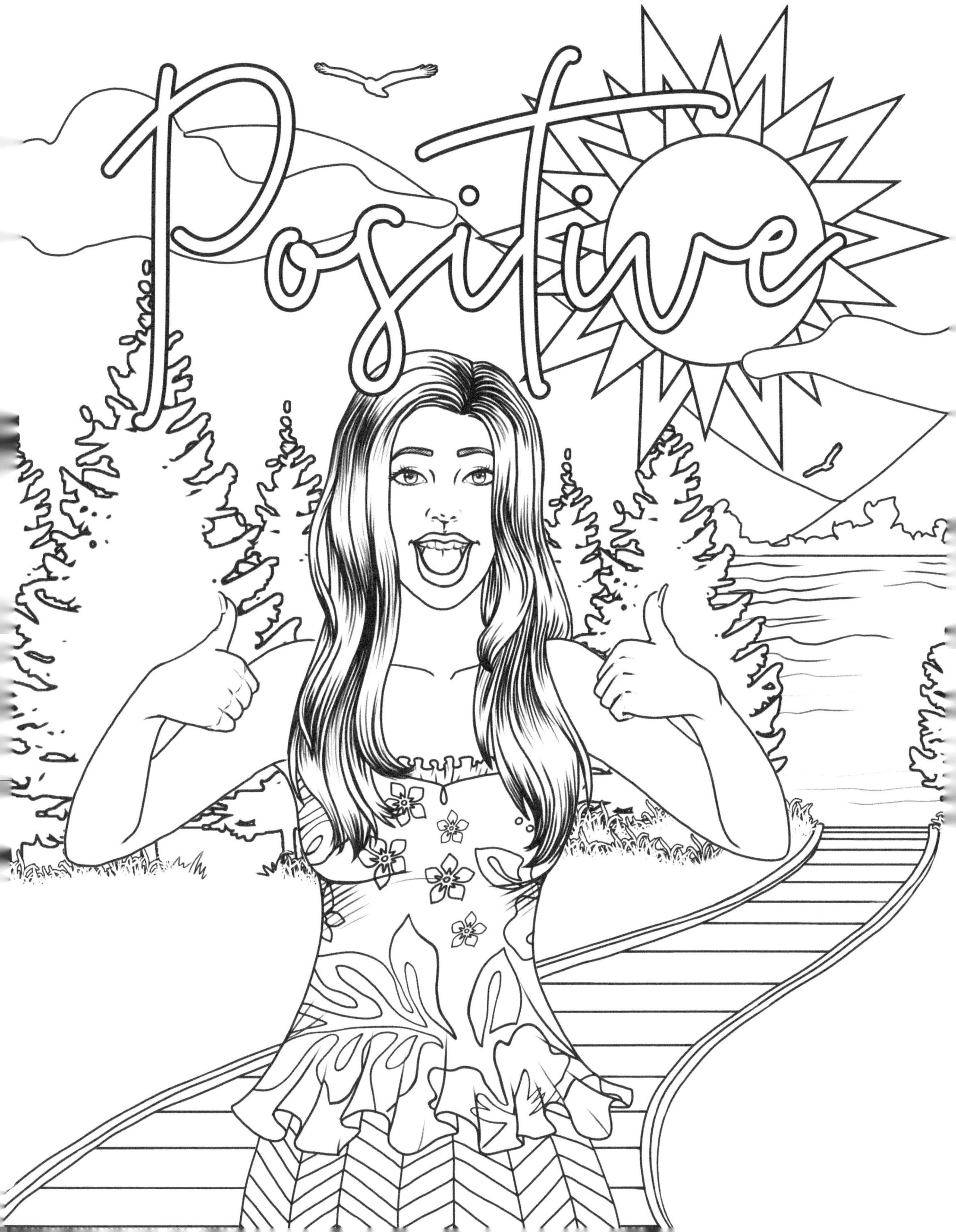
Positive

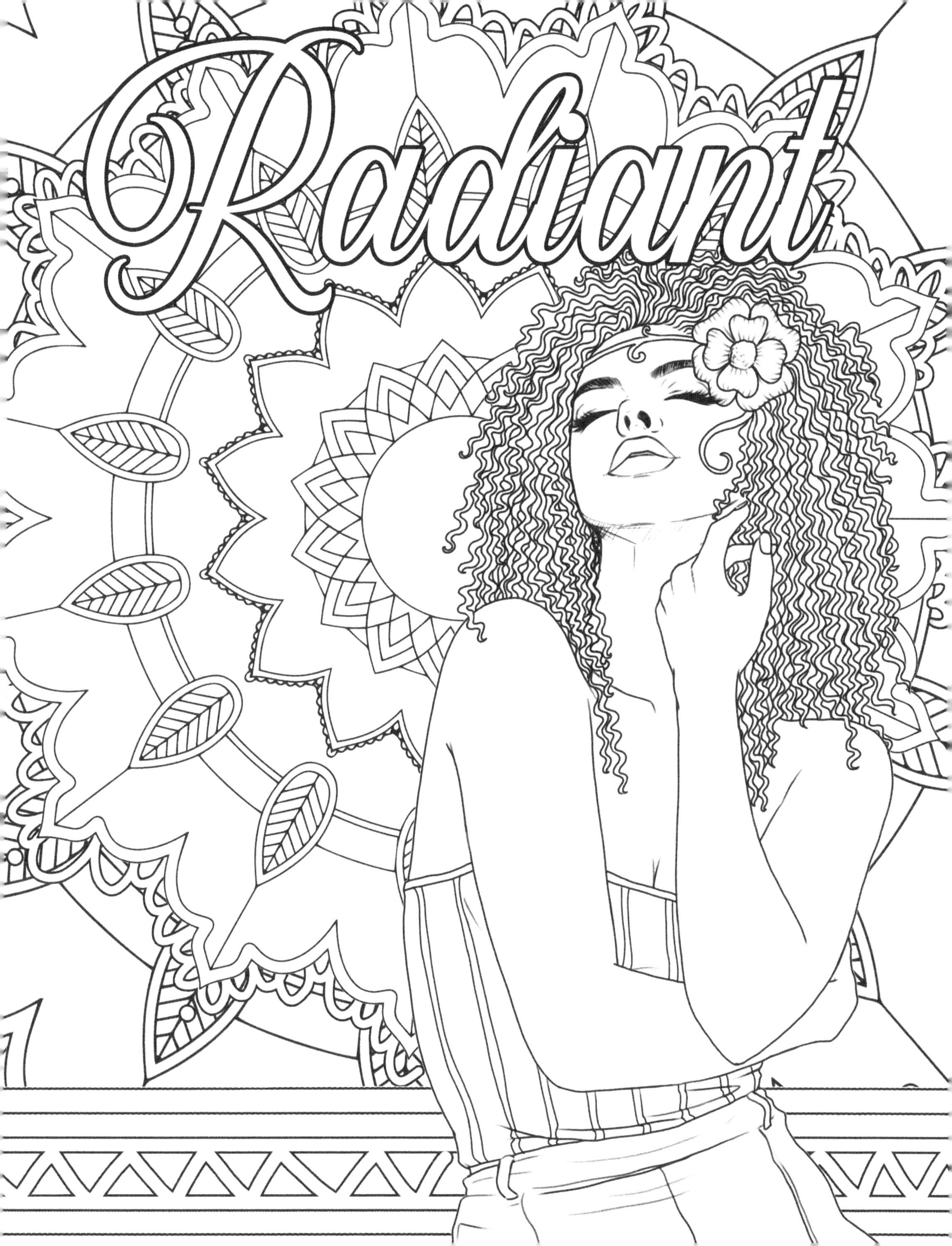
Radiant

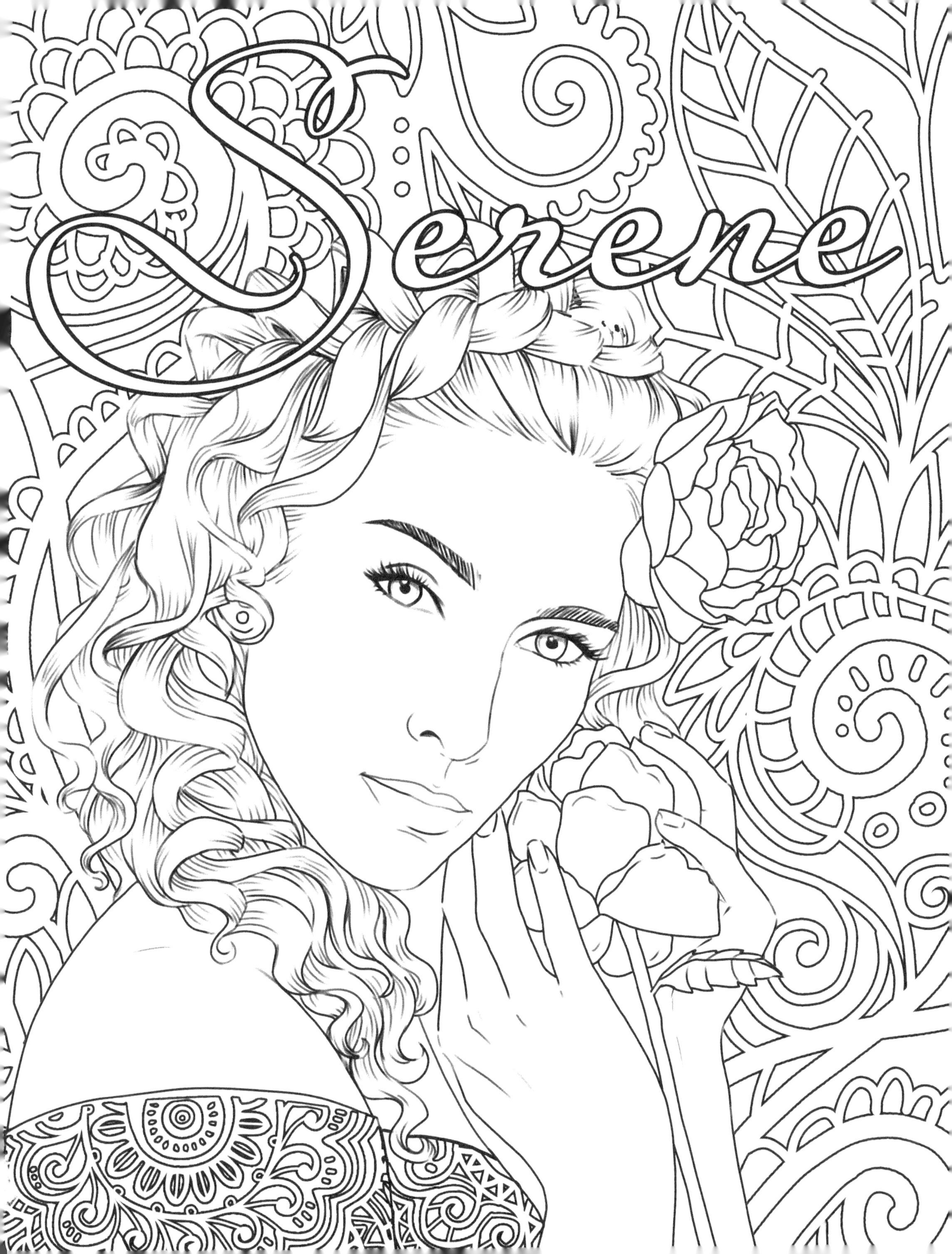
Serene

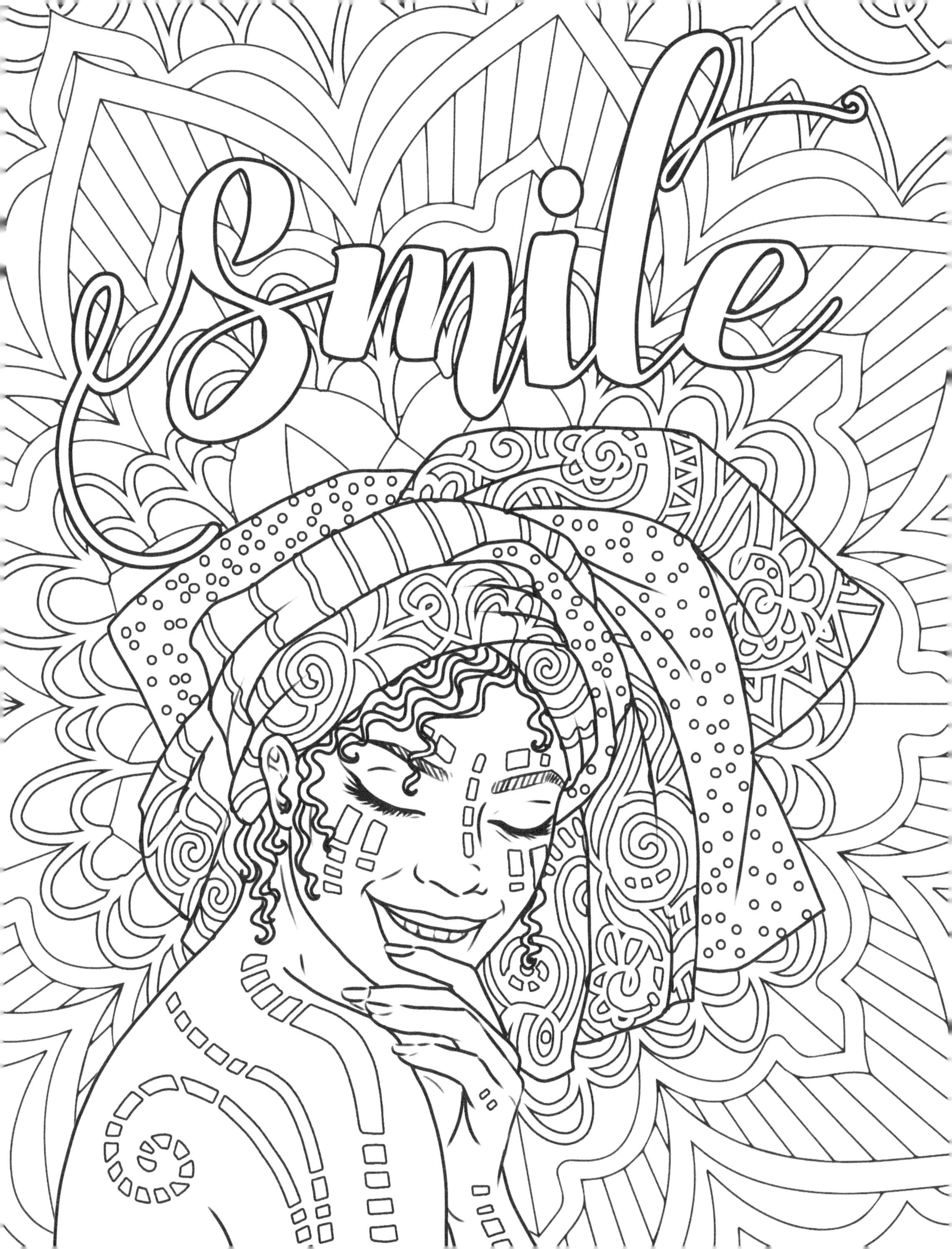
Smile

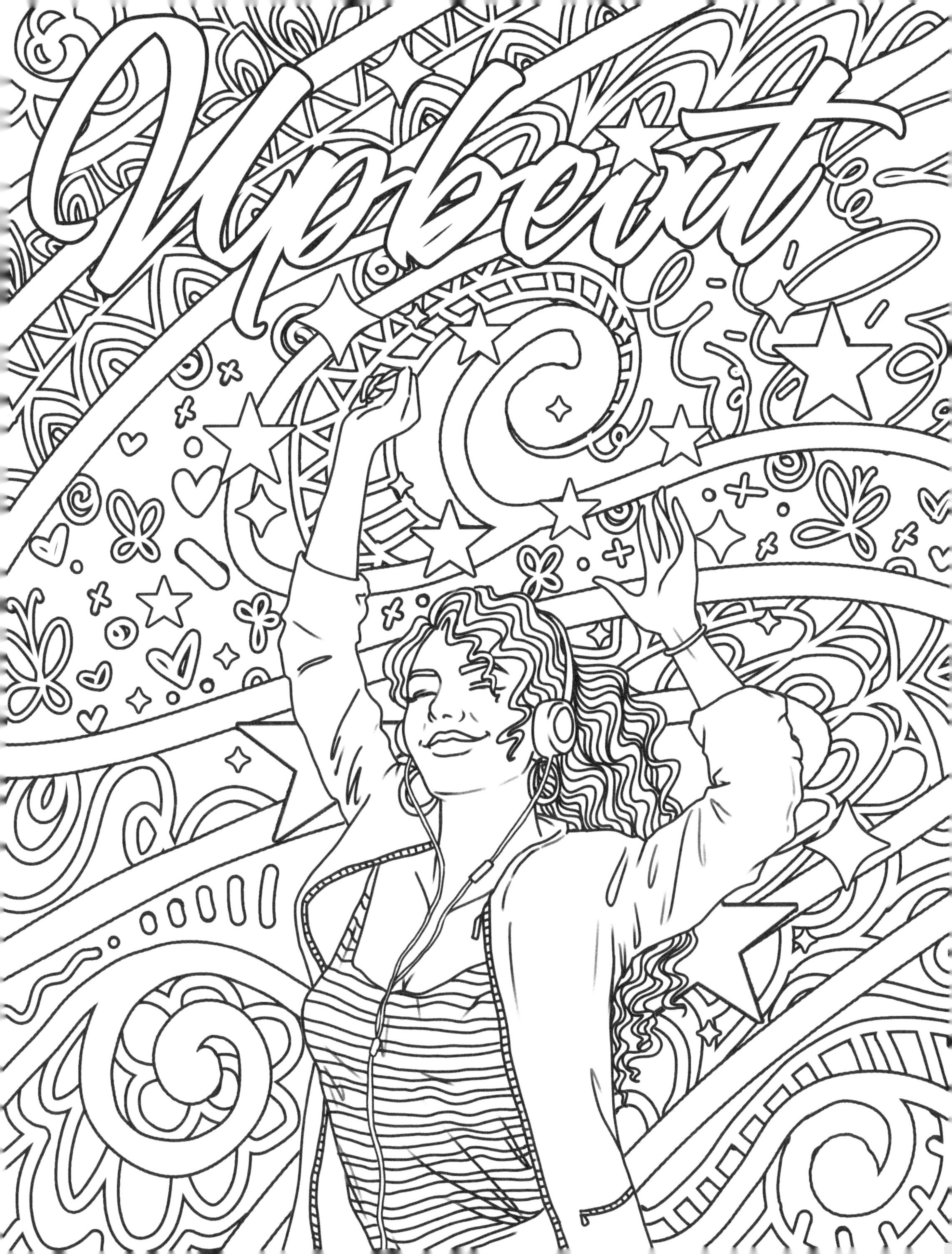
Upbeat

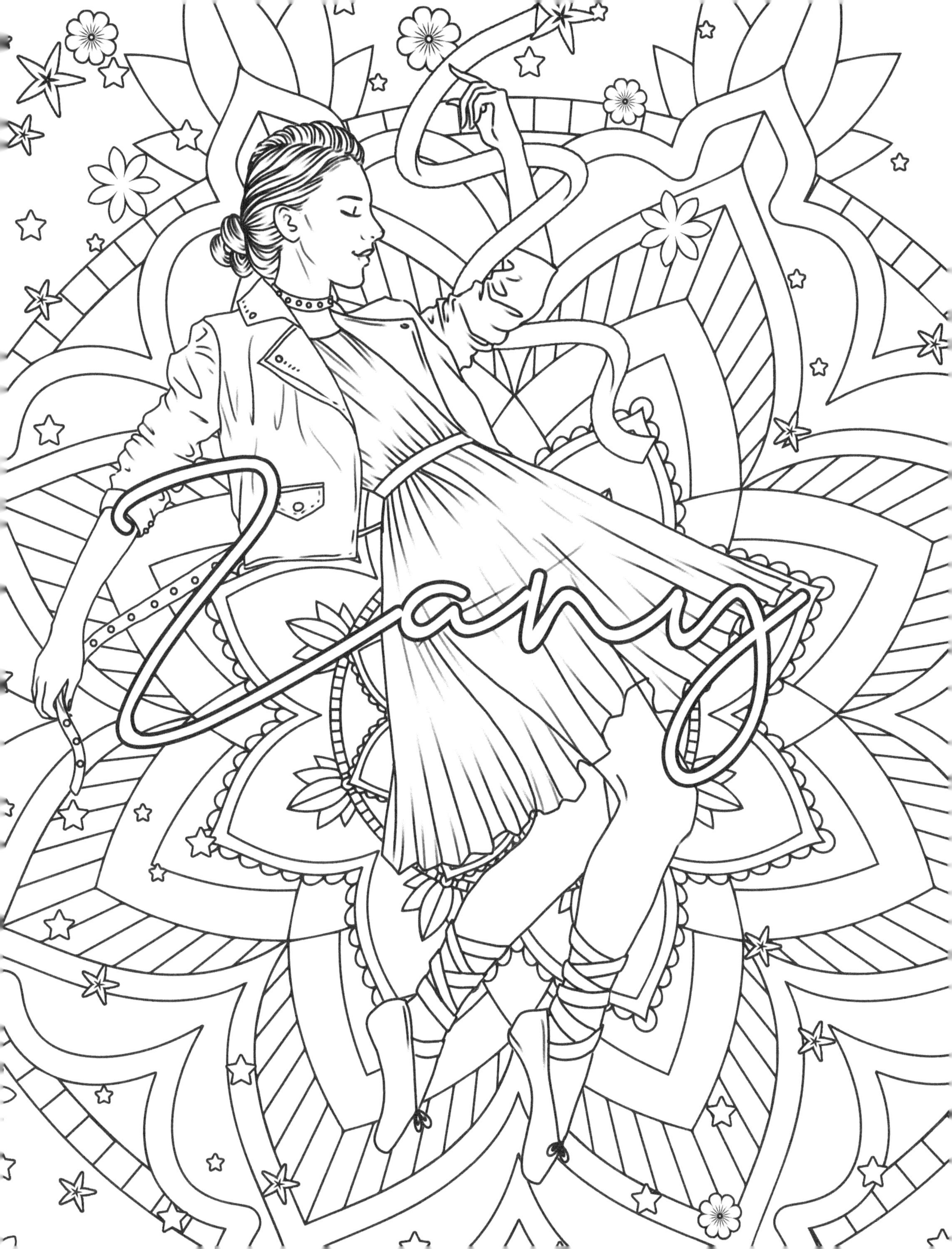
Zany

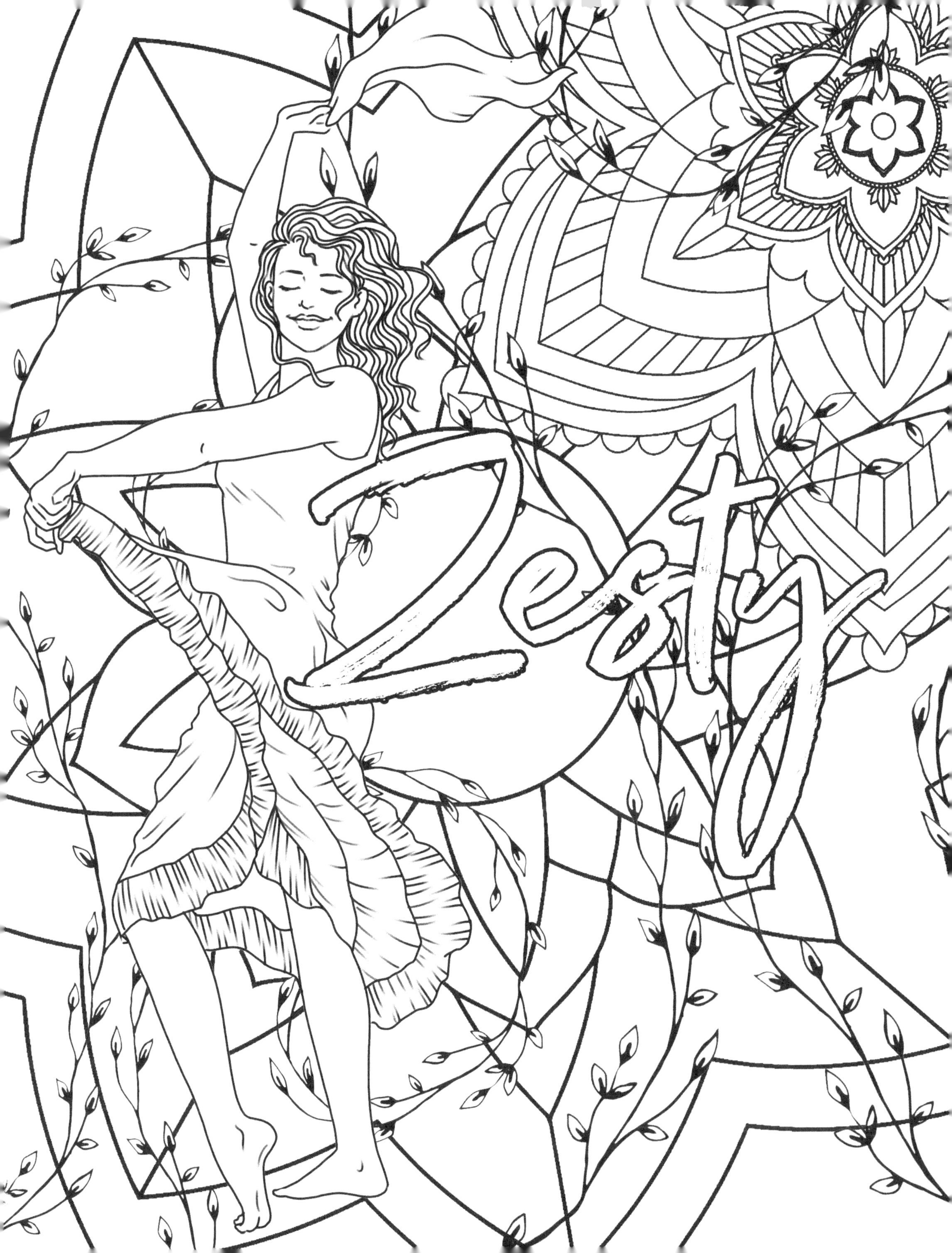
Zesty

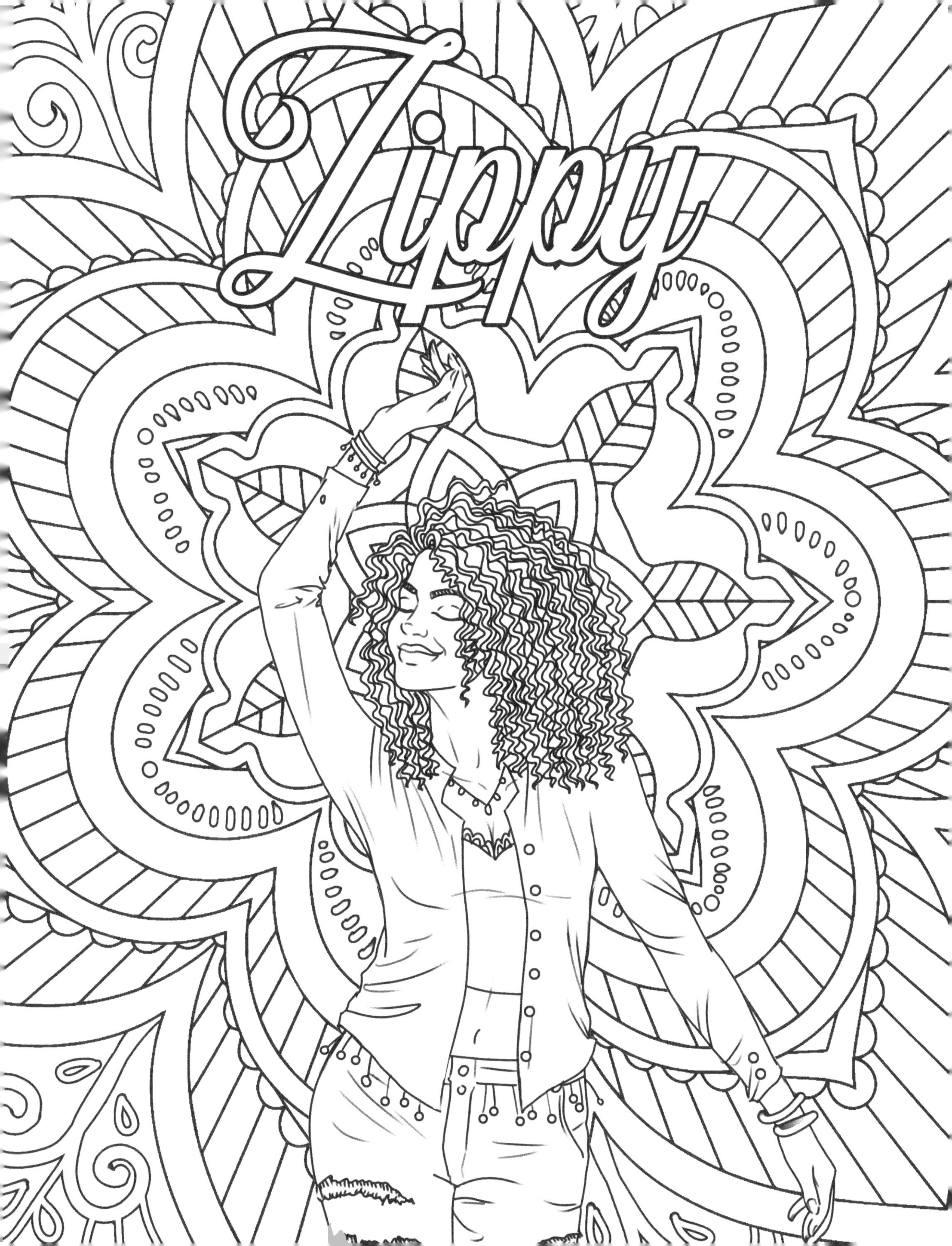
Zippy